THE GREAT WHITE
SHARK SCIENTIST

THE GREAT WHITE SHARK SCIENTIST

TEXT BY **SY MONTGOMERY**

PHOTOGRAPHS BY **KEITH ELLENBOGEN**

Houghton Mifflin Harcourt
Boston   New York

ONCE AGAIN, AND ALWAYS, FOR DR. MILLMOSS. —S.M.

TO MY LOVING NIECE, MAYA, AND ALL CHILDREN IN A
HOPE TO INSPIRE SHARK CONSERVATION AND AWARENESS
OF THESE MAJESTIC ANIMALS. —K.E.

Text copyright © 2016 by Sy Montgomery
Photographs copyright © 2016 by Keith Ellenbogen

www.hmhco.com

The text of this book is set in Amity Jack, Flood, and Latienne.
Maps on pages viii and ix © NOAA
Shark illustration on pages 11 and 40, and dingbats throughout by Mariah Mordecai
Maps on page 57 © MA Division of Marine Fisheries and Ocearch

Library of Congress Cataloging-in-Publication Data
Montgomery, Sy, author.
 The great white shark scientist / written by Sy Montgomery.
  pages cm. — (Scientists in the field)
 Audience: Ages 10–14.
 Audience: Grades 7 to 8.
 Includes bibliographical references.
 ISBN 978-0-544-35298-8
1. Skomal, Gregory—Juvenile literature. 2. Marine biologists—United States—Biog-
raphy—Juvenile literature. 3. White shark—Juvenile literature. 4. Wildlife conserva-
tion—Juvenile literature. 5. Marine resources conservation—Juvenile literature. I.
Title. II. Series: Scientists in the field.
 QH91.3.S575 2016
 578.77'092—dc23
 [B]   2015003494

Manufactured in China
SCP 10 9 8 7 6 5 4 3 2 1
4500573062

CONTENTS

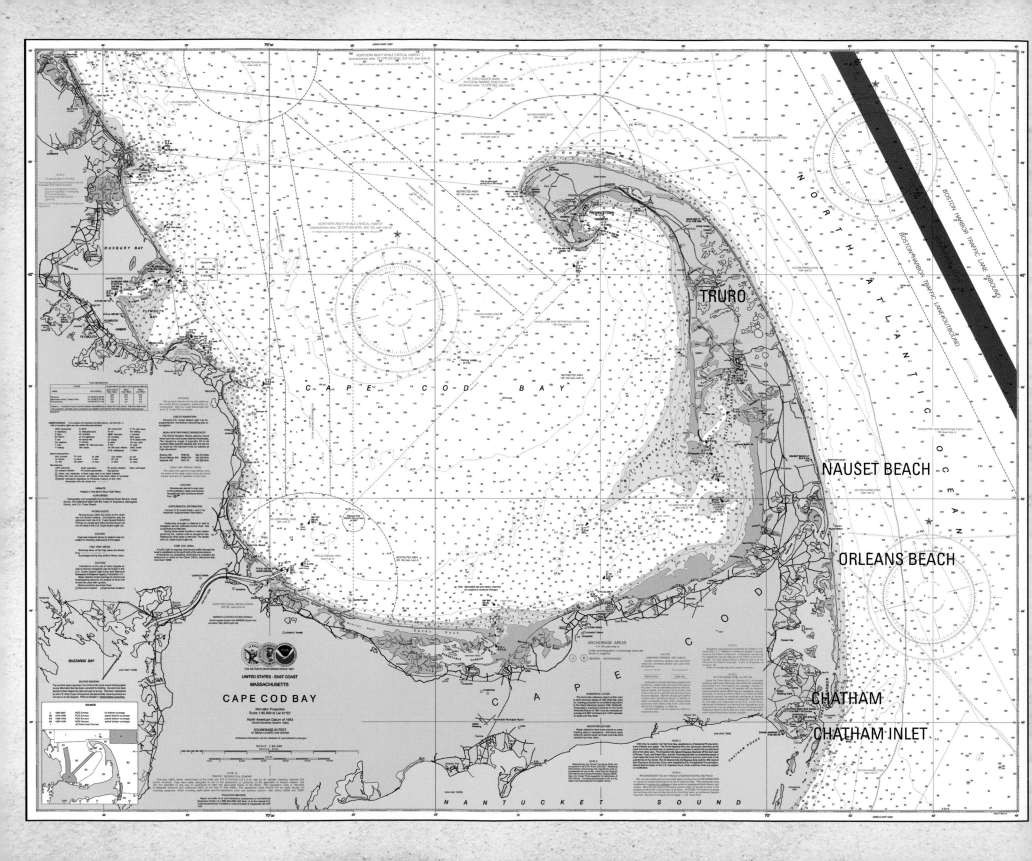

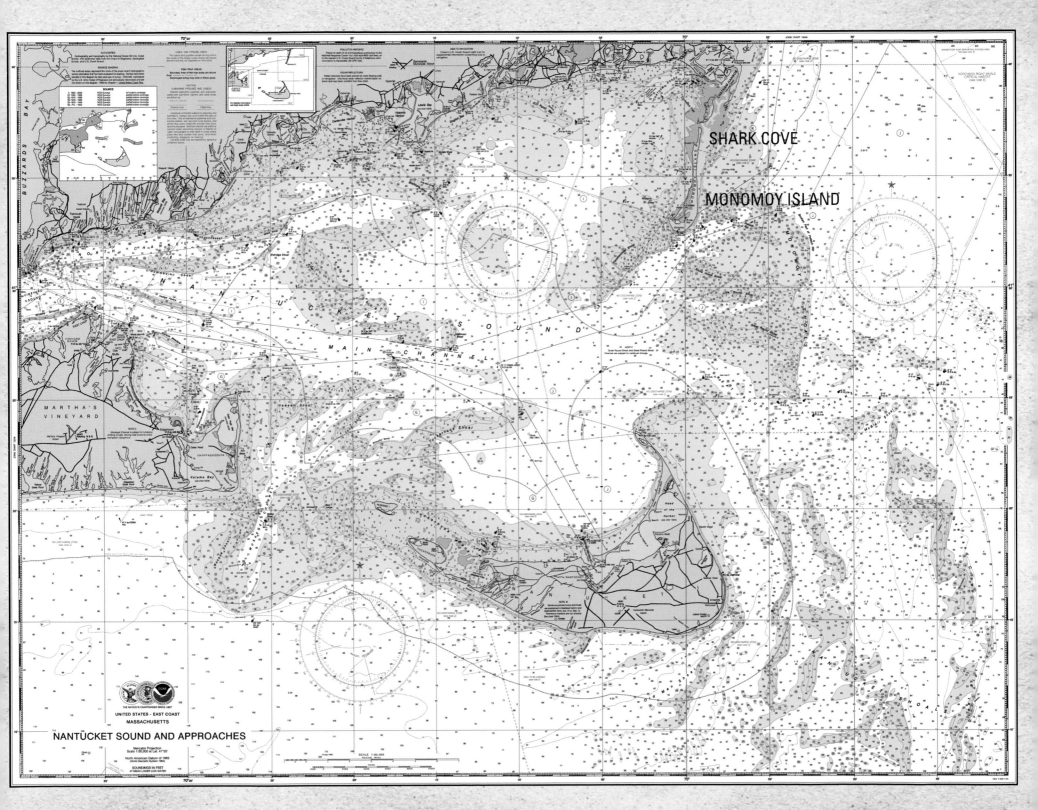

SHARK COVE

MONOMOY ISLAND

BUZZARDS BAY

MARTHA'S VINEYARD

UNITED STATES - EAST COAST

MASSACHUSETTS

NANTUCKET SOUND AND APPROACHES

Mercator Projection
Scale 1:80,000 at Lat. 41°25'

North American Datum of 1983
(World Geodetic System 1984)

SOUNDINGS IN FEET
AT MEAN LOWER LOW WATER

SCALE 1:80,000

CHAPTER 1

TUESDAY, JULY 8

"It's pretty treacherous right here," says Greg Skomal, a fifty-two-year-old great white shark biologist with the Massachusetts Division of Marine Fisheries. But he's not the least bit nervous. Piloting the twenty-four-foot powerboat *Aleutian Dream* through the shallow, six-foot-deep channel of murky green water at Cape Cod's Chatham Inlet is risky business—but skipper John King is up to the task. No, Greg's got only one concern today. Though in the thriller film *Jaws* (shot not far from Chatham on Martha's Vineyard), everyone worried about seeing a great white shark, Greg is worried about the opposite. He's worried about *not* seeing one!

Greg knew he wanted to be a shark biologist since he was in eighth grade, growing up on Long Island Sound, watching Jacques Cousteau's adventures on TV. In Greg's thirty-nine years on the job, he's always had plenty of sharks to study. New England's waters host two dozen species of sharks, from the strange-looking, schooling scalloped hammerhead to the spiny dogfish, a small shark caught here mainly to ship to England

for fish and chips. But recently—within the last decade—Cape Cod's marine ecology has dynamically changed. Now, each summer, just as the beach-going season begins, the Cape's cool waters are attracting new visitors: the most powerful, storied, and mysterious of all sharks—and the sharks who are also the most misunderstood.

"Great whites are not at all what people say about them," Greg stresses. "They're not hyper, all curmudgeonly and angry and wanting to kill something. They're not like that at all! I've *never* met one like that.

Greg Skomal, shark scientist.

They're laid back. They're calm. They're beautiful." In fact, great whites are Greg's favorite sharks. And now, finally, he has a chance to study them—practically in his own backyard. His big smile, flashing as bright as the reflection of sun on waves, shows he's relishing the adventure.

Great whites live all over the world's cool and tropical seas, but until recently were best known from off the shores of California, South Africa, and Australia. This season, with a team of volunteers, Greg begins a new study of the great white shark population off Cape Cod. His plan calls for eyes both on the sea and in the sky. Working with a spotter plane flying overhead, Greg hopes to locate great whites and then get close enough by boat to take video of them so he can iden-tify individuals. In this study, taking video is more important than tagging sharks. "Ultimately," he explains, "the goal is to determine who's out there, and whether we've seen them before. The more we know about individuals, the better. We need to spend time getting the demographics of the population, such as male or female, size and age."

How many great white sharks are swim-

The wind was perfect for kite-surfing—not flying or boating.

ming off Cape Cod's famous beaches? Maybe more than most people think. Though in recent summers sightings have prompted beach closings several times a season, Greg thinks that great whites could be harmlessly passing near busy beaches remarkably often, unseen and unsuspected. Greg estimates that his study will take three years to find out.

But studying great whites isn't easy—especially today.

"Chatham Inlet is a pretty dangerous area on a normal day," Greg tells us. "And this isn't a normal day!" Until just an hour ago, the National Weather Service had a small-craft advisory in place. To even attempt to find great whites, the weather has to be good enough so that both the spotter plane and the boat can go out. Wind, rain, and fog will scuttle an outing. Waves make the job harder: they crinkle the water's surface and stir up sand from the bottom. "You can be right over a shark and not see it," Greg says. And when a shark is spotted, waves make it difficult to keep the animal in view—and exceptionally difficult to film it.

But according to the weather forecast, today may be our best shot all week. We had hoped to go out yesterday, but the winds were too high. Flags, awnings, and Fourth of July bunting snapped and billowed on shore, whipped by twenty-two-miles-per-hour winds. Conditions were perfect only for kite-

Wayne Davis with his single-engine Citabria.

surfers. By the end of the week, the forecast was for weather even worse.

So on this Tuesday morning in early July, Greg had resolved to try again. At the Chatham Fish Pier, he had gathered today's team: our skipper, John King, and his wife, Pam, who live here in Chatham and own the *Aleutian Dream;* Cynthia Wigrin, the founder of the Atlantic White Shark Conservancy, which funds Greg's great white shark work; and Jeff Kneebone, who was a student of Greg's at the University of Massachusetts,

working on a Ph.D. on sand tiger sharks. So that I could write this book for you, they let me come along, with the photographer Keith Ellenbogen to take these pictures.

John gives the safety briefing: Life jackets are located in the starboard (on the right when facing forward; "port" means on the left) compartment. He points out the two fire extinguishers. Only three people at any given time are allowed on the observation platform above. "And when we are working on a shark, do not stand right in front of me," he

Tides constantly resculpt the Cape's coast.

maneuver the *Aleutian Dream* expertly, coordinating with Wayne's instructions from the air. And on board the boat, Greg will have to keep even with his subject, holding the video camera steady at the end of a long pole stuck in the water.

Why go to all this trouble? Because each shark looks different. Some have distinctive scars or notches on the dorsal fin or elsewhere on the body. But these features change as a shark ages and acquires more injuries—which is apt to happen if everything you eat, you must first kill with your face. What always stays the same on a great white, Greg explains, is the individual pattern along the shark's left and right sides, where the dark upper (or dorsal) surface meets the white underparts—especially around the "chin," gills, and base of the tail. The team needs to get footage beneath the shark, too. The only way to tell the sex of a mature shark is to check under the tail. A male will have two long, trailing cylindrical organs called claspers; a female will not.

Capturing all this on film, admits Greg, "presents massive logistical issues. But we're good at overcoming these things," he says with another big smile. "We think of them as challenges."

These are challenges everyone seems eager to meet. The Kings love sharks so much

cautions—because then the captain can't see. "We'll try to get back by three p.m. Drink water. If you have sunscreen, put it on."

The good news is, despite the wind, the spotter plane has already managed to take off. At nine a.m., spotter pilot Wayne Davis had texted Greg with the news: Flying at 1,200 feet in his light single-engine, two-seater Citabria (spelled backwards, that's "airbatic" to showcase a plane as agile as an acrobat), Wayne saw a shark he estimated to be nine feet long about a quarter mile off the beach, in eight to ten feet of water. "We

might as well mobilize and give it a shot," Greg decided. So in spite of the weather, we set sail at 10:15 a.m. We'll head south and west toward Monomoy Island, until we get more news from Wayne. "It's ugly out," Greg said, "but we might as well go out there and try."

Studying great white sharks is tough on even a calm day. These powerful fish can be remarkably shy. They spook easily. In order to get the kind of video Greg needs—clearly showing the shark's entire body, including both sides and bottom—John will have to that not only do they let Greg borrow their *Aleutian Dream*; John has specially modified it for Greg's study. They've outfitted their boat with a "pulpit"—a slender, gangplank-like metal platform with a metal railing, so that Greg can stand or even lie on his belly just feet above a shark to record a video of it, or attach a telemetry tag to its dorsal fin. "John's boat is a new boat for us," Greg explains. In the past, they've used a commercial harpoon fishing boat as well as some of the state's smaller vessels. "We're still sorting out the methodology," Greg shouts over the motor while we cling to the railings and the boat gallops over the chop.

Finally, John slows down so Greg and his fellow shark expert Jeff can ready the gear. Using electrical tape, they affix an underwater GoPro camera, used for extreme action videography, to a lightweight aluminum pole normally used to extend the reach of house painters. Three other GoPros will be mounted directly on the boat to film the shark from above. "It's fun," says Greg, "to figure out what might work."

Now seems a good time to check in with Wayne again on the radio. Typically, the pilot flies a regular route for Greg, looking for seals and sharks from south to north, to the tip of Cape Cod. "I've made a few passes," he says. "Visibility is surprisingly good. It

could be better, but it's not bad." He's seen no sharks since that first one, though he's still looking.

At 11:15, we approach Monomoy Island, an eight-mile spit of roadless, sandy land off the mainland. "Look at all those rocks!" says Keith, marveling at what look like the hundreds of dark boulders on the beach. "Those aren't rocks," says Greg. "Those are seals—lots of seals!" Cynthia, Jeff, and Pam set to counting them. It looks like there are 250 just in this one group. "The sharks eat everything," explains Greg, "but it's these seals that's drawing them to the Cape."

Gray seals, once abundant in New England waters, had been all but exterminated here, victims of bounty hunters who killed them, believing (incorrectly, scientists now confirm, by analyzing seals' stomach contents) that they competed with fishermen for their catch. Actually, seals mostly eat sand eels, which fishermen ignore. But thanks to the Marine Mammal Protection Act of 1972, the seals have staged a comeback. From a few dozen gray seals first spotted in the early 1990s, the Cape's population has grown to more than 15,000. And their favorite "haul-out," where they leave the water to rest, sun, and reproduce, is here on Monomoy.

The Cape gets three other species of seal visitors, but the gray seals—misnamed, as

Chatham's busy harbor.

only the females are mottled with gray; the males, weighing up to eight hundred pounds, are jet black—are favorites of adult great whites. Greg calls these marine mammals "Scooby snacks." A single seal, with loads of nutritious blubber, could satisfy a great white's appetite for more than a week.

Though some swimmers might be alarmed to know great whites are cruising close to tourist beaches, they come here to eat the seals, not the people. Great whites aren't man-eaters, Greg stresses. "More people are injured by their own toilets than by great white sharks," he points out. (Think about it: tiny children can fall into the bowl and drown; you can slip on a wet bathroom floor and bonk your head on it; there is even a theoretical risk that your toilet could explode!) Great whites rarely hurt humans; in the past hundred years only fifteen great white shark attacks were fatal. In fact, in U.S. waters, there have been only a little over a hundred unprovoked great white shark attacks in the past century—averaging only one a year. By contrast, more than 200,000 Americans are injured in toilet-related accidents each year.

Still, a bite from a shark is no fun—especially if the shark in question is someone who can grow twenty feet long, with three hundred razor-sharp, serrated teeth capable of severing an eight-hundred-pound seal's head in one chomp. But this makes it all the more remarkable that most of the few people bitten by great whites survive. Why? Because when this shark discovers its mistake—that it's bitten a human and not a seal—it almost always spits the person out: *Pthh!*

A visitor from Colorado discovered this firsthand when he was bitten on the leg in July 2012 off the Cape's Ballston Beach in the town of Truro. He was swimming more than a hundred yards out from shore and was near some seals. Though the wound was serious and bloody, the shark bit only once, and the man swam back to shore, unhappily but unassisted. Within six months, his injured leg had healed so well that he was back to biking and running.

That was the first great white shark attack on a person in Massachusetts in seventy-six years. Greg doesn't want to see more. That's one reason his work is so crucial. "Knowing more about this species will help protect human beings," says Greg. "We could really get a sense of when sharks are around beaches and when they're not."

But equally important, says Greg, is that his work will benefit the great white sharks themselves. Nobody knows how many great whites remain, but scientists agree that shark numbers worldwide are dropping alarmingly, as people catch them for their fins and teeth, for trophies, and sometimes kill them out of sheer ignorance and spite.

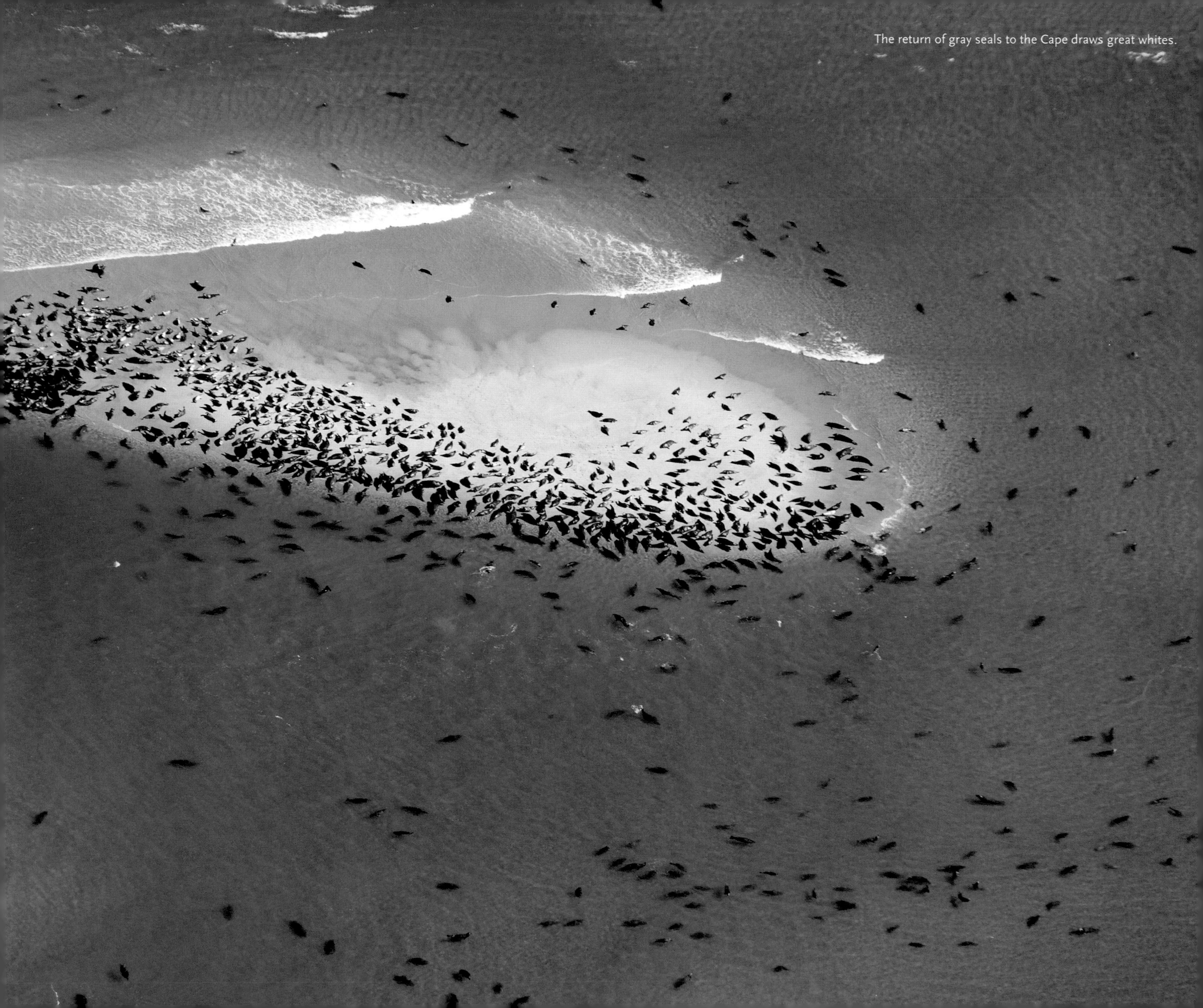
The return of gray seals to the Cape draws great whites.

"I want these animals to survive," says Greg. "They control the balance of the ecosystem." Great white sharks are apex predators—carnivores with no natural predators of their own. They directly affect not only the prey they eat, but also the creatures who their prey would eat. Taking out sharks causes ripples all the way down the food chain. In Australia, for example, researchers found that a sharp decrease in the shark population caused an increase in the kinds of fish that the sharks usually preyed upon. These fish then ate so many algae-eating, smaller fish that algae began to smother the coral reefs. And a 2007 study found that on the eastern coast of the United States, thirty-five years of large shark decline led to increases in the number of rays and smaller sharks—including cownose rays, who ate so many scallops that the scallop fishery collapsed. And since scallops filter debris from

Caught in a fisherman's net, this seal faces a tragic, slow death.

seawater, even the quality and clarity of the seawater suffered.

Discovering great whites' many secrets will be essential to protecting the health of the oceans. "And in order to put in place the rules and regulations that allow for the survival of this species," says Greg, "we really need to know about the animal and how it lives from day to day."

Greg carefully notes the number and location of the seals on his sightings form. How does the behavior of seals correlate with the behavior of sharks? This is just one of the questions he hopes his studies will eventually answer. He scans the seals with binoculars. Have any been bitten by sharks? "If we see

shark bites, Jeff and I will man the GoPro poles and see what we get," he says.

Sure enough, he finds two wounded seals. But they weren't hurt by sharks. They have gillnets stuck on them, possibly dooming them to lingering deaths. "People try to rescue them, but it's hard to do," he says, shaking his head. The seals always flee from their rescuers. "Better to be eaten by a shark."

By the time we reach the tip of Monomoy, it's 12:30, and fog begins to roll in. "It happens quick in these parts." Wayne's voice crackles on the radio. "I'm going to have to land."

"We don't have sky power," Greg sighs, "so we might as well head in too." He's frustrated, but remains optimistic. "We're doing

pioneering stuff. We never had predictable access to white sharks in the western North Atlantic—and because of all these seals out there, now we do.

"The complications come from factors we can't control," he explains. "Weather. Sharks . . ." And there's another complication too: the sharks leave the Cape in the autumn. "We have to smash a whole year's worth of study into just two months," Greg says.

Happily, the summer's still young. July and August still stretch ahead of us. "I know the sharks are out there," Greg promises as John docks the *Aleutian Dream* back at the Chatham Fish Pier. "All we have to do is find them."

Gray seals.

WHAT IS A SHARK?

"Sharks aren't fish; they're monsters."

"Sharks are man-eaters."

"Sharks all grow to huge size."

All false!

Here's the truth: Sharks are fish. There are about five hundred species of sharks, and of these, only three species—the bull shark, the tiger shark, and the great white shark—are responsible for two-thirds of all shark attacks on people. Only six percent of the five hundred shark species have ever been known to hurt humans. Most sharks are harmless, small animals. Most shark species grow only three feet long.

Sharks belong to a group of fishes called Chondrichthyes (Kon-DRICK-thees). This scientific class is named for the Greek words for "cartilage" (*khondros*) and "fish" (*ikhthus*). Sharks and their flattened relatives—the rays and skates, and the strange, shark-like, deep-sea chimeras—all have skeletons made entirely of tough, flexible, lightweight cartilage, like we have in our nose and ears and between our joints. This feature gives them the same benefits as balsa wood gives model airplanes. Unlike most bony fish, they don't have swim bladders to keep them afloat. These fishes' scales are also different: they feel prickly like sandpaper, and are called denticles (DENT-ih-culls, from the Greek word for "tooth"—in fact, if you looked at these scales under a microscope, they'd resemble teeth). All Chondrichthyan fish have teeth in their mouth, too, and these are unique. They're lined up in replicating rows.

Within this larger group of more than a thousand fish species, the five hundred or so who are sharks all share a similar, torpedo-like body shape, rigid dorsal fins, and five to seven paired gill openings through which they breathe water. But in other ways, the various species of sharks are "as different from one another as tigers and hedgehogs," as one researcher put it. They range from the six-inch-long spined pygmy shark, with a glow-in-the-dark belly, to the largest fish in the ocean, the polka-dotted, filter-feeding whale shark, who can stretch forty-five feet long and weigh 47,000 pounds.

Sharks are ancient fishes. They date back to the early Devonian period, about four hundred million years ago. By the Carboniferous period, three hundred million years before *T. rex* appeared on land, sharks ruled the seas. They included some bizarre models. Some had teeth on top of their head. Others had spiraling lower jaws and whorls of teeth coiled in a spiral like a circular saw.

The biggest predatory fish to ever live was a creature many consider to be the direct ancestor of today's great white. *Carcharodon megalodon* (car-CAR-oh-don meh-GAL-o-don, from the Greek words *carcharos* for "ragged," *odon* for "tooth," and *mega* for "big") lived from about twenty to two million years ago. Its triangular, serrated teeth grew seven inches long. Megalodon could bite six times harder than today's great white, whose scientific name is similar: *Carcharadon carcharias* (*carcharias* also comes from the Greek *carcharos*).

Based on the size of the teeth, researchers speculate that Megalodon grew as long as a high school basketball court is wide and weighed forty-eight tons; its mouth stretched six feet across. Some people think there may be some Megalodon sharks still out there, undiscovered, in the ocean's depths, but, alas, most scientists agree that this giant is long gone. Greg dismisses the idea as "wishful thinking." It might be exciting to think of Megalodon out there, but the great white shark, largely unchanged over millennia, is perfect in design—and that's shark enough!

FIRST DORSAL FIN:
The great white's is typically quite large.

EARS:
Labyrinths embedded in the skin inside the head provide directional hearing underwater, allowing some sharks to hear the low-frequency sounds of struggling fish 820 feet away.

SKIN:
Covered with toothlike denticles to resist water turbulence and protect from parasites and predators.

AMPULLAE OF LORENZINI:
(am-PULE-eh of Loren-ZI-ni) These fluid-filled sacs are organs that detect close-range electromagnetic fields generated by beating hearts, breathing gills, or moving muscles—as well as the earth's distant magnetic field, which sharks may use to navigate.

CAUDAL FIN:
Most sharks have an elongated upper tailfin and a smaller lower one, but the great white's is more symmetrical, like that of a tuna, allowing it to swim quickly with less effort.

NOSTRILS:
These help detect scent from miles away. One quarter of a shark's brain is devoted to smell.

SECOND DORSAL AND ANAL FINS:
The very small fins improve the flow of water across the tail, reducing drag and helping it swim more than fifteen miles per hour. Though not as fast as a mako or marlin, the great white shark is a very efficient swimmer.

TEETH:
The great white's twenty-four upper and twenty-four lower teeth are exposed in the front ranks, with about 250 others lying in wait in back rows that move forward to replace lost teeth like a conveyor belt. At any one time, a third of a great white's teeth are being replaced.

LATERAL LINE:
As in all fish, these pressure wave detectors run in a long line down the side of the body to help the shark sense water currents and pressure as well as their own posture and muscles as they swim.

JAWS:
During an attack, the great white lifts its snout and the lower jaw drops, and then the upper jaw protrudes, exposing the upper teeth. The upper jaw can be thrust forward from the roof of the mouth. (We can't do this because our jaws are made of bone instead of cartilage and are fused to our skull.)

CLASPERS:
Males alone have these paired organs, which they use in mating.

PECTORAL AND PELVIC FINS:
These help the shark stalk its prey slowly and imperceptibly.

GILLS:
Sharks must force water over their gills to extract oxygen from the water—either by drawing water into the mouth and over the gills, as nurse sharks do, or by swimming quickly, as do great whites and makos. Great whites die from lack of oxygen if they stop swimming.

PATTERN:
As individual as human fingerprints, the distinctive patterns where the dark and light parts of the great white meet help researchers identify who's who.

CHAPTER 2

WEDNESDAY, JULY 9

Up a set of wooden stairs at the Chatham Fish Pier, there's a deck where tourists and locals hang out, forearms on the rails, watching the scene. Fishing boats stream in, trailing an entourage of birds. Men in bright yellow and blue rubber overalls are gutting their catch and tossing the leftovers to eager gulls and seals.

"The seals are making a comeback!" observes a grandfather in a yellow Ohio State cap. His grandson, a tot dressed in a *Sesame Street* T-shirt, jumps up and down and claps at the sight of a curious female gray seal who's cruising the docks, looking for a treat from the fishermen.

"But they're drawing the sharks!" says

Seagulls fly over a fishing boat returning to Chatham.

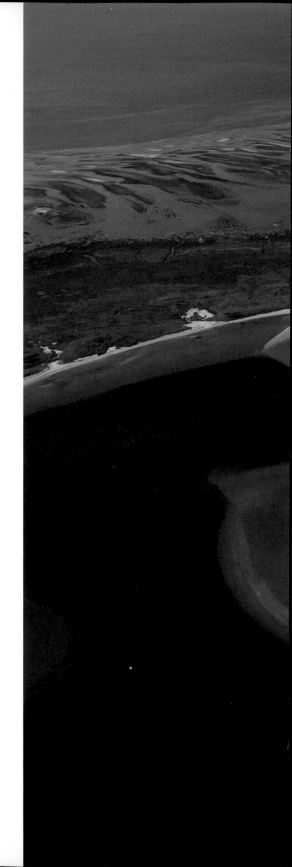

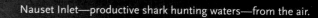
Nauset Inlet—productive shark hunting waters—from the air.

A gray seal looks up at tourists watching from the Chatham Fish Pier.

a lady from out of town, sipping a coffee. "Aren't you afraid of them?"

"Last year, we had several great whites we were all following," says a blond woman in seashell earrings. She's the little boy's mom, and has lived in Chatham for twenty-two years. "They're tagging them now with telemetry. One of them is off Florida now. It's so cool to keep up with them! I'm glad they're here."

Keith and I have joined the crowd as we wait for another cell phone call from Greg. At 9:40 this morning, he had called to tell us Wayne can't fly due to clouds. But there's a saying here in New England: If you don't like the weather, wait a minute. It's that changeable. We hope the clouds will clear—and if so, we can join Greg on the water to look for sharks.

Greg calls again at 10:30: "We may have Wayne go up and do his transect—but we gotta catch the tide. I'll be right over!"

Because Pam and John are away and the *Aleutian Dream* is unavailable, this time we'll be taking a smaller boat, one of the state's fleet of twenty, which is stored a short drive away at Stage Harbor. Greg pulls up in his white Division of Marine Fisheries Super Duty Ford truck to take us there, where Cynthia and Jeff are waiting for us.

This boat is a twenty-one-foot Maritime Skiff, a utilitarian craft used for everything from water quality sampling to fish studies. But with no pulpit, "it'll be a bit of a challenge," as Greg puts it, to film or tag a shark if we find one—if we go out at all.

Since 2009, when he became the first scientist to successfully satellite tag a great white shark in the Atlantic Ocean, Greg and his crew have outfitted thirty-nine sharks with different kinds of telemetry on their dorsal fins. Thirty of them have acoustic tags. These communicate with twenty-eight receivers on detector buoys set up around the Cape. When a tagged shark passes near one of the receivers, the tag "logs in" much like the way a worker "punches in" at a factory, recording the date and time the shark appeared, again and again until it leaves.

Twenty-one of those sharks also have pop-up satellite tags. These are data loggers that pop off the animal after a period of months, float to the surface, and transmit to a satellite that calculates its location. Bigger migratory patterns can emerge from these data: a shark tagged off Cape Cod in August may be in Florida in February.

And there are five great whites who have real-time satellite tags, which means each time one of these sharks surfaces, it transmits its location to a satellite. (Though sharks breathe through gills, so they don't need to surface for oxygen, they come up to catch prey such as air-breathing seals.) There's even an app you can download to follow these sharks on your cell phone!

This summer, Greg hopes to tag more sharks. But more important, he's after good video identification of the sharks. "We don't want to tag a new shark until we know who it is," says Greg.

At 11:25 a.m., we learn that Wayne has taken to the air, so we take to the sea. It's low tide, and Greg must pilot the boat carefully. The depth sounder shows we're in ten feet of water . . . then six feet. Then four. Each new storm can cut fresh channels, pile up unexpected sandbanks. "I haven't run the channel with this new cut, so it'll be an adventure," says Greg. "Worst case scenario," he jokes, "is we get stuck and we get out and push. That would really suck. I hear there are great whites out here!"

Carefully Greg steers us into deeper water. The depth sounder now reads twelve feet. Overhead is a sun halo—a sort of round rainbow. A lucky sign. "I have a good feeling about today," Greg says.

Above us and to port we can see Wayne's Citabria. "You see us down here, Wayne?" Greg asks on the radio. "What are your conditions?"

The pilot Wayne Davis and photographer Keith Ellenbogen in Wayne's Citabria. Wayne took this photo with Keith's GoPro.

"Beautiful!" Wayne replies. He heads off for his regular transect to try to find us a shark, while we continue south toward Monomoy.

The weather has turned fine. But the glare from the sun on the water is ferocious. "You want no swell, no surf, good water quality—and sometimes even that's not enough," says Greg. "There could be a shark right under us and we wouldn't know it.

"Sharks are very dynamic," he continues. "Some stay in a given area for hours. Some for a day. Some don't." The tagging data has provided some intriguing insights.

Mary Lee, for instance, a sixteen-foot, 3,456-pounder (she was hauled from the water and weighed!), has logged more than 16,000 miles in the two years since she received her real-time satellite tag from Ocearch, a nonprofit collaborating with Greg and other shark researchers around the world. But Lydia, another shark with a real-time tag, "makes Mary Lee look like a real homebody," Greg says. Tagged in Jacksonville, Florida, in March 2013, this fourteen-foot, 2,000-pound shark has traveled more than 25,000 miles, swimming from Cape Cod to Georgia, then Mississippi—and then due east, in eight days crossing half the Atlantic. Two weeks later she was back in Florida.

Katherine, weighing in at 2,300 pounds, is another Ocearch animal, tagged off the Cape in August 2013, and one of Greg's par-

Cape Cod is famous for its many lighthouses.

ticular favorites. She's traveled more than six thousand miles since then, down the East Coast through some of North America's busiest tourist waters. "She shows up here every year," Greg says, "but she's late this year."

Cynthia checks Katherine's coordinates on www.ocearch.org with her smartphone. "She's south of Cape Hatteras right now. But she's headed our way."

Each shark is an individual, with individual secrets to share. "Julia has some interesting habits," says Greg. "She's another one of our favorites. We've developed a history with both these fish; the longer we know them, the more we like them." Since she was outfitted with an acoustic tag in 2011, Julia has returned to the Cape four years in a row. She's one of the first sharks to arrive each year, which they know from the receiver buoys. "Knowing she's back is like seeing an old friend after a long winter," he says. But they never see her, and she's shown no particular pattern to her travels once at the Cape.

"We love Curly, because she's a big shark," Greg continues. She was seventeen feet long when he tagged her in 2009, nine miles east of here, while Discovery filmed her feeding on a dead whale. Her pop-up tag revealed she had traveled from the Cape all the way to the Sargasso Sea—in the middle of the North Atlantic. Nobody saw her again until September 2013, when the team took GoPro footage and recognized the black and white pattern on her gill slits while reviewing it. She had grown to eighteen feet. "Curly's out there somewhere," said Greg. "We hope she comes back."

At 11:20 a.m., we reach the southernmost tip of Monomoy. We pass its desolate lighthouse, deactivated after a century of service. The beach, too, is deserted. All the seals are somewhere else today. Why? Wayne calls on the radio. "I'm almost finished with the transect," he says. "Where are all the seals?" He can't find any either. And where are the sharks? Are they out there somewhere, hunting the seals?

"Who knows? There may not be many sharks around. I'll have Jeff go up top," Greg says as we steam forward. Despite the iconic image in movies and art, it's surprisingly rare to see a great white's dorsal fin. (Why? Turns out they can get sunburn!) Greg has only seen it two or three times. What Jeff will look for is a shark-shaped shadow in these green murky waters. "If he sees it, we'll stay right next to it and see if we can film it."

But no sharky shadows are in the offing today. Just green water and bright glare. And ahead, as we arrive at an area called Southern Cove, we spot a welcome, bright yellow sight: one of Greg's twenty-eight detector buoys. It's held in place by a hundred-pound mushroom-shaped anchor, which digs into the sand, connected to thirty feet of heavy chain.

If we can't find a shark, at least we can see if the buoy did. Greg and Jeff strain to haul up the eighty-pound buoy labeled C-3. Cynthia hands a magnet to Greg, who touches it to the buoy, allowing it to download its data so it can be transferred to Cynthia's laptop.

In theory, the receiver records any animal with an acoustic tag that comes within five hundred yards of it—and that includes seals and thousands of other fishes that other researchers are studying, as well as Greg's sharks. "We've got something!" Cynthia announces. "Tag number 28367 registered on July 7 at twelve twenty-seven. Then it hung around till one. Then it was here from two forty p.m. to two fifty-two."

But with thousands of animals out there in dozens of studies, who is 28367? Is it a seal, a fish, or a shark?

Greg could figure it out when he gets back to his data set in his office. But there's one person who can tell us now: John Chrisholm, a big, bearded shark expert who's worked with the state fisheries department for twenty years. John had decided to be a shark biologist in kindergarten, and thereafter made his parents take him to the New Eng-

The team syncs the receiver buoy to Cynthia's laptop.

land Aquarium at least once a month. He's on shore leave with a back injury (the result of pulling up one of these buoys)—otherwise he'd be out here with us. Cynthia texts him, and within a minute comes the reply: 28367 is Salty—a twelve-foot female first tagged in August 2012. She was last detected off the Cape on October 23, 2012—and was detected off Cape Canaveral in Florida in March.

"Salty! Oh, that's great!" choruses the crew.

Wayne calls in on the radio. "Is that you hovering over that buoy, Greg?"

"Yup. You seeing seals anywhere?" asks Greg.

"The ones at the southern end of the cove are all in the water," Wayne reports.

"Good to know," says Greg. "We'll kick around another hour and see what we've got here."

Searching, searching . . . approaching Chatham Inlet, we check in with Buoy A1. Cynthia reads the data as it pops up on her laptop screen: "30047 . . ." It sounds familiar. "That's a bass," she remembers. But there's another detection recorded: 28367! "Salty was here too! Between one forty-one and one fifty-three." By checking just two buoys, Greg now has a map of where Salty traveled and when during the hours of

12:27 and 2:52: between Southern Cove and Chatham Inlet and back again.

It's just a tiny piece of the puzzle—a puzzle as big as the North Atlantic Ocean. But that's how puzzles are solved, and how science gets done: piece by piece. Even seeing no sharks today is progress. For in science, "zeros are okay," says Greg. Negative data is still data—and data is what every scientist is really after.

CHATHAM REALLY LOVES ITS SHARKS!

When *Jaws* was filmed four decades ago, the fictional town fathers in the movie tried to keep their great white a secret. They were afraid the news would kill the tourist industry.

But today, the great white has been rebranded. Chatham, where the winter population of 6,600 people swells to 30,000 with summer tourists, proudly bills itself as the "Summer Home to the Great White Shark."

Evidence of shark pride is everywhere. Right across from the Coast Guard station, on the chainlink fence surrounding the entryway to the beach, you'll see plastic signs proclaiming CHATHAM LOVES SHAHKS (in the Boston accent) and inviting you to like its Facebook page, where you can find "everything about sharks happening in New England." Stroll down Chatham's Main Street and pop in just about any store: you'll find great white shark salt and pepper shakers, fridge magnets, swim trunks, belts, posters, greeting cards, dog collars, and

bottle openers. The Chatham Clothing Bar offers a wall of sharky T-shirts, sweats, and hats. One design proclaims EVERY WEEK IS SHARK WEEK. Another depicts the anatomy of a great white. A third shows the silhouette of the classic tall dorsal fin with the words THAT'S A WICKED BIG SHAHK!

While *Jaws* still plays twice a day during the summer at the Chatham Orpheum Theater, its executive director, Kevin McLain, explains that attitudes toward great whites have done an about-face

since the movie first aired. The late author of *Jaws*, Peter Benchley, was dismayed to learn of sharks' decline and became an ardent shark conservationist after his book was published and turned into a movie; his widow, Wendy, is president of the shark conservation group Shark Savers. In a line in the film, an official warns that yelling "Shark!" would provoke instant panic. "In Chatham now," says the theater operator, "you yell 'Shark!' in the middle of town, people come running *to* the beach, not away from it." On the Atlantic White Shark Conservancy's website, they've set the change to music: a soundtrack begins with the heart-thumping, spine-chilling theme from *Jaws* and then turns into Frankie Valli's love song "Can't Take My Eyes Off (of) You."

Not everyone is thrilled the sharks are here. Greg says he hears occasional grumbling from nearby beach towns. (Some people grouse about the seal comeback, too—despite the $1 million added to the local economy from tourists who come to the Cape for seal tours.) "Some would rather not know they're out there," Greg says.

When a lifeguard or beach-goer spots what's believed to be a white shark near the shore, the beach closes to swimmers—usually only for an hour or two. This typically happens fewer than a dozen times a summer across the entire Cape.

Most of the Cape's businesses, locals, and tourists seem to agree with Greg: "These iconic, wild animals are here," he says, "so why not celebrate them?"

Sharkabilia for sale in Chatham, proud home of the great white shark.

A great white shark swims toward two seals.

CHAPTER 3

MONDAY, AUGUST 25

On our next shark foray, we haven't even left the dock when Wayne, calling on Cynthia's cell, presents us with a tantalizing choice.

He's heard a report that a dead fin whale, who may be the third of its species to have died entangled in fishing gear on the Cape this year, was recently spotted ten to twenty miles from Chatham Harbor. Whale biologists are clamoring to find it again for study. But Greg is interested too. A dead whale is a banquet for great whites.

The day before, researchers at the Center for Coastal Studies in Provincetown had looked extensively for the whale carcass from both sky and sea. But they couldn't find it. Wayne wants to know: Should we leave the area and look for it today?

It's the end of August, the last week of summer. A lot has happened since we saw Greg in July. Most of that month was slow, but as August began, the team started spotting sharks in near shore waters on almost every trip. They've tagged two new sharks and videotaped many more.

But summertime is running out. When September arrives, sea winds will pick up and make shark sorties even more difficult. And the sharks usually leave the Cape around October on a mysterious migration Greg and other biologists are still trying to map and understand. Every outing is crucial to the success of the study; Greg can't afford to waste a day.

Greg looks up at Wayne's spotter plane, the shark team's "eyes in the sky."

John King expertly pilots the *Aleutian Dream* past treacherous sandbars.

"Let me talk it over with my team here," says Greg.

If we can find the dead whale, we might get a shark bonanza. Without the risk of hunting and killing, a whale carcass offers sharks a prize of nourishing blubber—enough to support several sharks. Dead whales may well have been white sharks' major food source before whaling nearly wiped them all out. Though white sharks usually travel alone (not even the mothers stay with their young), large numbers of great whites have been recorded feeding at one time on a single carcass.

But to reach the area where fishermen last saw the carcass would take several hours. And we might not find it at all. "It could shoot the day," says John.

"There could be ten sharks near the beach right here," says Greg.

In fact, just last Friday, the team identified *four* new sharks in the area we're consider-

ing leaving. The weather had been terrible; Greg lost his hat to the water as he squatted in the pulpit while waves pounded him. But with summer's clock ticking down, Greg had decided to go out anyway, and it paid off.

We decide to stick with the original plan and the usual study area—for now. "Roger that," Wayne replies on the radio. "I'm going to check the North End." While he runs the transect, we head south.

We're minus Jeff today, but besides Greg, John, Pam, and Cynthia, our team includes three others: Cynthia's bearded husband, Ben; a Chilean college graduate, Sebastian Kraft, who had worked off Chile's coast with Ocearch in March and April; and Jon Dodd, a shark biologist who later became a successful businessman, who now invests in socially worthy small companies. Sebastian has tagged makos and blues off Chile, but has never seen a great white. And as a volunteer with the National Marine Fisheries Services (NMFS) Cooperative Shark Tagging Program, Jon has tagged hundreds of sharks, but has only seen a great white once, fifteen years ago, off Montauk, Long Island, New York.

"We've had an easterly blow for a week. It'll kick everything up and makes visibility poor," Greg tells the eager crew. "But I have a good feeling. I think we'll get some action today. I *know* we will!"

Waiting for Wayne to spot a shark, we

check some of the receivers to see if any of Greg's tagged sharks have been in the area. At South Shark Cove, Ben hauls out the heavy buoy to download its info to Cynthia's laptop. Cynthia reads out the numbers: 25502 . . . 25437 . . . 25527 . . .

"No sharks!" she says, recognizing these numbers as assigned to other fish.

"It's an odd year," says Greg. "The sharks should be coming through here a lot. A very odd year!"

But wait—"28236," reads Cynthia. She remembers that number. "That's James!" she cries. "He came through at six thirty-six a.m. on August eleven, two weeks ago!" James, a sixteen-footer who may be thirty years old, was just tagged on August 8 with an acoustic transmitter.

"32307," Cynthia continues. She remembers that number, too. "That's Chex! He came on July twenty-seven at six forty-four a.m.!" Chex, a thirteen-foot male, was originally tagged on July 9, 2012, and he's been showing up a lot lately. Two weeks ago, Greg explains, he and his team were following a new shark, a female named Avery, who had been videotaped but not tagged. "It was really funny. We were following her all morning and getting all sorts of video on her," he says. With so much video evidence of this shark, she seemed a great candidate for tagging. "We would follow her for fifteen minutes, and then she would disappear, go deeper, come back in, and we'd find her," Greg says. "So what she did was, she disappeared on us. And then a shark pops up. And we tag it. It wasn't till we reviewed the videotape that we said, 'Wait a minute!' And then we found Avery again with no tag."

Soon they discovered what had happened: Instead of tagging Avery, they had tagged Chex!

Chex's original tag was set back a bit on his dorsal fin and was difficult to see. But his first tag was about to stop transmitting and fall off. They hadn't intended to tag him a second time, but Greg says, "It'll be good

that we did. Having long-term individual histories is important."

At eleven a.m., we check in at another receiver buoy. Chex was here on August 17 at 9:22. James cruised by on August 9, 10, and 11. We check a third receiver off Chatham Harbor: Chex came by last Saturday at 7:07 p.m.

"Sharks are in the area!" says Greg.

"32373 . . ." reads Cynthia. "Oooh! It's Curly, on the twenty-third!" A whoop goes up from Pam, John, and Greg. "Oh, great!" says Pam. "I'm so glad she's alive and well!" This is the first they've heard from her since 2013.

"Let me check again to make absolutely sure," says Cynthia. In the sun's glare, the last digit of the number looked like a 3—but was really an 8. This animal was not Curly; it was a bass.

But here's other good news: Julia was in town! On July 2 she pinged in at 11:17. And another shark, 32310, checked in . . . but who? As John continues to pilot the boat, the rest of us are huddled around Cynthia's computer to find out—when we're interrupted by a burst of sound from the radio. It's news from Wayne.

"We've got one!" yells John. "Hold on!" He guns the motor.

A great white shark near the surface.

"One hundred yards," says Wayne on the radio. "Nine o'clock!" The shark is ahead and to the left, about where the nine is on the face of a clock. "Nine thirty now, John, if you want to get a little closer."

Greg picks up one of the poles to which he's already attached a GoPro, and rushes to the pulpit. Ben grabs another and stands on the foredeck.

"Forty yards, ten thirty," says Wayne. "Eleven o'clock, about five boat lengths . . . now three boat lengths . . ."

Is the shark we're following already tagged, or is it new? Cynthia drops in the hydrophone, an ultrasonic telemetry and tracking receiver attached to a long black wire, to

A depth meter on the *Aleutian Dream* warns of dangerous shallows.

see if it can pick up a signal. All the acoustic shark tags transmit at the same frequency—sixty-nine kilohertz—but each has a distinctive pattern of eight or nine pulses. This is an individual coding scheme, sort of like Morse code, identifying each individual shark.

"No signal," she reports. "It's a new one!"

"He's down on the bottom!" shouts Greg. "What's the depth?" he asks John.

John checks the depth meter on the boat. "Sixteen feet down," he reports.

"He swam right by us!" Greg calls out. He plunges in the GoPro and lets it swing along in the water. "I've got him!" he shouts. "One o'clock! He's down there—big shark, big shark!" Greg estimates he's at least a twelve-footer. "See him, John? Now dead ahead. He's right under me. Yikes!"

Wayne's voice comes in on the radio with a report from the sky: "He's going toward the shoals. Go back to starboard. Two boat lengths now . . . give it a jab of power, John."

"He's eleven o'clock, ten thirty—one boat length . . ." says Wayne.

"We got a visual," says Greg. "Let's stay with him—see if he goes toward shore . . ."

And now the shark dives.

"What's the depth?" asks Cynthia.

"Fourteen feet of water," replies John.

"He's staying right down there," says Greg. "He's dead ahead! Right under me!"

Now that Greg has video, this shark would be a good candidate for an acoustic tag. Attaching it to a shark's dorsal fin involves a small harpoon, but it's not like harpooning a whale. "I think of it as sneaking up on someone and piercing their ear," Greg says. It probably doesn't hurt the shark that much, and may sting for only a few seconds. But the information these tags provide could be lifesavers for the species. The data from the tags will alert the world if these sharks' numbers are decreasing—and if so, provide insights into how to help.

Cynthia assembles the tagging pole, screwing together four three-foot lengths of hollow metal. Greg attaches a dart to the end and holds the tag flush to the pole with three rubber bands. He returns to the pulpit. Now if only the shark will come closer to the surface.

"C'mon, buddy!" calls Keith.

"Periscope up!" says John.

"Rise!" pleads Pam.

The shark starts to move. "Up on the shoal," Greg directs John, "a little more to port . . ."

And it disappears. "He's not stupid, is he?" says Greg. "The old sneak-out!"

But then, another message on the radio from Wayne:

"I've got another one! About a mile away."

The question is: Do we stay with the shark we have, or go after the new one?

MORE THAN ONE WAY TO TAG A SHARK

Greg with tagging pole.

As well as tagging white sharks on the Cape, Greg also tags other species of sharks—and there are different ways to do this. Here, rather than tag the shark in the water, Greg and colleagues haul the shark aboard their vessel so he can place a real-time satellite transmitting tag by hand on the dorsal fin of a mako shark. Once the shark is released, every time it surfaces, the tag will come out of the water and transmit to a satellite, which will calculate the shark's position. This is the same kind of tag used on the white sharks Lydia, Katherine, Mary Lee, and others, who can be tracked by Ocearch.com's Shark Tracker. This photo and those on the following two pages were taken off Montauk, Long Island, New York.

Greg bolts a real-time transmitting tag to the dorsal fin of a seven-foot tiger shark. This one was named Big Kahuna. You can follow his path on the Ocearch.org Shark Tracker!

ABOVE & BELOW: Big Kahuna's tail was tied to the boat so he'd hold still for the tagging—and then he rushed away (right toward Keith!) when he was released.

ABOVE & BELOW: Big Kahuna swims away with his new tags. He also has a conventional yellow tag that is an additional identification marker—like a serial number.

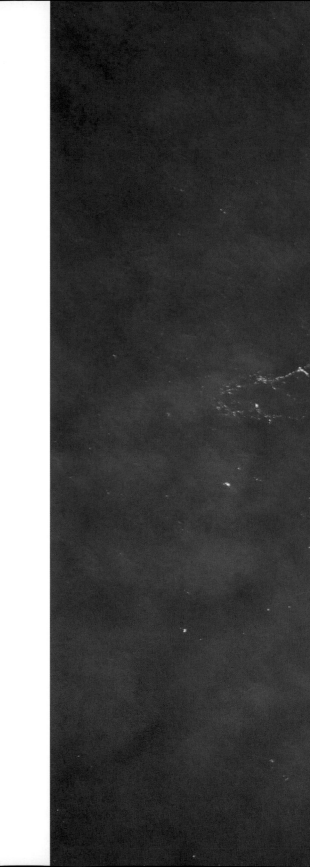

CHAPTER 4
LATER THAT SAME DAY

"Want to make the move?" Greg asks the team. Video is even more important than tagging on this study, he reminds us. So, as noon nears, we head after the second shark.

As we approach South Beach, Wayne tells John to slow down. "He's dead ahead. Thirty degrees starboard. He's probably going to swim . . . no, nine thirty, a boat length—he's coming right to us!"

Cynthia plunges in the hydrophone. She listens for two full minutes. A transmitter, if there is one, should ping every ninety seconds. But there's no signal. "Another new one," Greg announces. "Sweet!"

The shark stays calmly near the surface while Greg and Ben take video. They get images of the sides, top, and bottom.

"Nice! Nice! No tag, and he's pretty mellow," Greg says. This shark seems like a fine candidate for an acoustic tag—and conveniently, the tag is already loaded onto the harpoon. "Let's keep an eye on him," Greg says to John. "We'll follow him a little. Don't get too close."

"Eleven o'clock, six boats." Wayne's voice crackles over the radio. Jon calls the information out to Greg up in the pulpit.

"He's in the deep," reports Greg. The tagging harpoon won't reach. But Greg is patient. "He'll be there for quite a while. There's not a hurry till we get him to a spot that's perfect for us," he says.

Cynthia drops in the hydrophone to listen: Is there a new shark in the area?

From his plane, Wayne can see the shark even better than the crew can from the boat.

Greg on the pulpit, taking video.

"Starboard, couple of boat lengths . . ." Overhead, Wayne continues to guide John as they follow the shark.

Ten minutes later, the shark is still too deep to tag: The *Aleutian Dream*'s depth meter reads seventeen feet. And then, he's gone.

But soon Wayne spots him again. "He's a quarter of the way to the beach. John, you got him?" he radios. This beach has no people on it—and no seals, either, only cormorants, big black diving birds who can arrow through the water. "He's heading toward the shoal," Wayne reports.

A shoal—a sandbank under the water—could be good luck for us. If the shark swims over it, he might be in water shallow enough for Greg to tag him. "Good," says Greg. But then he reconsiders: "Well, I don't know if it's good." A shoal is a navigation hazard; the *Aleutian Dream* might get stuck on it.

John's depth meter reads nineteen feet, eighteen feet, sixteen feet . . . five minutes go by. We see the shark almost straight ahead! But it's still too deep: twenty feet. "I can hardly make him out," says Greg. "C'mon up!"

"I've got another one," says Wayne, reporting a *third* shark! "What would you rather do—tag this one, or take a look at that one?"

"Is this one coming up on the shoal?" asks Greg.

Indeed it is—and Greg wants to stick with it.

The second shark disappears. Wayne can still see the third one, though. "He's coming up on the sandbar," he reports. Cynthia eagerly drops in the hydrophone—and confirms this one is new too. But as sudden as a shiver, the third shark vanishes into the dark water.

"We've lost them all, haven't we?" asks Greg. At least now, at 1:20 p.m., he has a moment to eat the peanut butter and jelly sandwich he packed for lunch.

But just as Greg takes his first bite, Wayne calls again. "I've got two of them! One's at ten thirty and four boats, going toward that sailboat there. It's deep. I don't know if you can see him."

We're now just at the edge of Shark Cove. It's aptly named: this is one of Greg's most productive study areas.

"Got sight on both of them, I think!" calls Greg. "But one's off in a trench, and I can't see him well. The other one was at one o'clock."

Again, Cynthia plunges in the hydrophone. We all listen. No sound. One or both of the sharks could be the ones we spotted earlier today—or they could be new sharks nobody has met or video-recorded before. There's no question they're worth pursuing.

Now Wayne calls on the radio to report that one of the sharks might not be a shark

after all. In the Cape's soupy green waters, even eyes in the sky can't always tell a sharky shape from a dark patch or a big fish such as a swordfish, or even a tight school of tiny fish called menhaden.

But wait—that dark patch wasn't a shark, but now he sees two sharks for sure!

Almost straight ahead, we see a triangular fin: tall, dark, and classic—this is exactly the sort of sight that would prompt a town to close a beach to swimmers. "Give it a little power," says Wayne to John. As we approach, the fish to whom the fin belongs is right at the surface, and we get a great, close look. It's not a shark at all!

It's a four-foot-long ocean sunfish, also known by its scientific name: *Mola mola*—*mola* means "millstone" in Latin. This harmless jellyfish-eater can grow to two thousand pounds and is one of the strangest-looking fish on the planet: It looks like a big round swimming head with two giant fins. It doesn't even have a tail, which it lost in the course of its evolution, but swims by waving its tall dorsal and big anal fins in a sculling motion, turning like the oars on a rowboat in a figure eight. It's called a sunfish because it likes to sunbathe near the surface, where its tall dorsal is often mistaken for a shark's.

This is not the same animal Wayne has spotted. "It's two boat lengths ahead, on your starboard," Wayne declares over the

Greg films a great white with the GoPro.

radio, "and it might be hard to see—it's heading right into the sun!"

"Got it. Going left!" cries Greg as he and Ben lower the GoPros. The shark swerves away from Greg's camera—and beelines for Ben's! "He came right at the camera!" Greg calls to Ben.

At this point, Cynthia deploys another tool on board—a decoy. Created in South Africa in the shape of a baby seal, it's made of foam held together with plastic and wire ties, covered in gray carpeting, and attached to a long rope. "Throw it out!" Greg calls. The decoy might entice the shark to stay nearby while Ben and Greg film it. The shark swerves. Cynthia retrieves the decoy and throws it again. But the shark doesn't seem interested.

At 1:30, the shark finally disappears. "That was awesome!" says Greg. He's sure they got great video—and it should be fun to watch the shark lunge for Ben's GoPro. Greg celebrates by taking another two bites of his PB&J. Before he can take a third, Wayne's on the radio again: "Two sharks here!" he says. John pushes the throttle: "Hold on!" he tells us.

We catch up to the two sharks in minutes. It's an embarrassment of riches: one shark to port, another to starboard. "You want to listen or look?" asks John. Greg feels we should listen first. John cuts the motor so Cynthia

can listen on the hydrophone. No signal. "So pick one to follow," says Wayne.

Ben hardly has time to charge up the battery to one of the GoPros before a shark is dead ahead, almost right under Greg.

"I got him!" calls Greg.

A big swell rolls toward us—Greg's eyes are on the shark. "Can you ride this one?" asks John. Of course he can. Squatting, he dips his knees like a surfer on a wave.

"He's a little guy," Greg says, observing his

quarry. "Little" in this case means he's only eight to ten feet long, and perhaps "only" nine hundred pounds. The little guy weighs as much as a full-grown moose. "He's definitely a new shark," he says to us.

And he's shy. He doesn't like the boat, and he doesn't like Greg's GoPro. He tries to get away. "No, you're not chickening out on me!" says Greg to the shark. But the small shark escapes, and we can't seem to find him again.

No matter. Wayne's on the radio again

Sharks are difficult to see in the Cape's green, murky waters.

Between shark sightings, Greg records notes on his data sheet.

almost immediately. "Come over here, half a mile. We got another one at ten o'clock," he reports.

"This GoPro's full," announces Ben. "Got another one?" Keith offers his.

"Where's the fish?" asks Greg. "One o'clock," answers Wayne. "And it looks nice and shallow," adds John.

This is a much bigger shark, and actually seems interested in our boat. Why should sharks approach boats anyway? Perhaps, muses Greg, the shape and size of the boat, from the perspective of a shark beneath

it, reminds it of a dead whale. Or perhaps sharks are just curious. "There's so much about them we don't know," he says.

Pam calls out: "Here he comes! Right under the pulpit!"

"Great!" says Greg. "I think I got it. Got some good pictures of that one!"

Wayne calls in with more news: Marshfield Beach just closed because of a shark sighting there. "Big ones in the bay!" says Greg. (Later we discover it was a sunfish.) But Wayne has his eyes on two more sharks—maybe three! The area he's watching is a

short flight but a twenty-minute boat ride away. Finally, Greg will get a chance to finish his sandwich.

When we get to Wayne's new site, Cynthia drops in the hydrophone. This time, she gets a signal. The pulses match acoustic tag number 32307. "Chex is here!" she cries—the thirteen-foot shark tagged on the last day of July instead of Avery. "I've missed that shark!"

Another shark is about eight boat lengths ahead, at roughly five o'clock. Wayne directs John while Greg mans the pulpit with the GoPro. "Ten thirty, three or four boat lengths. You're converging. Come starboard a little—now dead ahead."

"We got him! Thanks, Wayne," says Greg. "I've got him! Big fish! Big boy! A fourteen-footer—that's the winner of the day!" says Greg.

As he films the shark, Greg can see some distinctive markings. This big shark has a bite mark on the dorsal fin. It is not only *not* a tagged shark; it's definitely not one of the others we've already seen earlier today, but a shark entirely new to the study. "We'll just stay with it and see . . ."

Jon Dodd, the shark biologist from Rhode Island, knows exactly what Greg is thinking. "I've put the tagging pole behind you, Greg."

We're in seventeen feet of water, too deep to tag. "C'mon over!" Greg calls to the shark. The great white comes up on our port side. We can all see the dorsal fin, a rare sight, and its wound, completely healed. We wonder: Who would dare bite a great white?

A seal would, answers Greg, if it was fighting for its life. Or another shark. Larger sharks are known to eat smaller sharks. (And some kinds of sharks, including sand tiger sharks, even eat each other in the womb, eating most of their brothers and sisters before they are born!) Researchers studying other shark species have seen males biting each other as they fight for the right to mate with a female. This may be the

case with great whites, too—though nobody knows, since their mating has never been observed. But in the shark world, mating gives new meaning to the words "love bite." In the species in which mating has been observed, researchers notice that females get badly bitten. "Sharks have no hands, so they have to hold on with their mouths," Greg points out. In some shark species, females actually have thicker skin than males to help them survive their suitors' attentions.

Greg can now see that this shark also has another healed wound on its right side. It's a C-shaped scar—in the shape of open shark jaws.

The big shark dives again. "One more rise and we'll have him," says Greg.

"C'mon—please come up!" begs Pam.

We're in twenty-two feet of water now, and Greg loses him—for the moment. "He faded down into the dark water," says Greg. "But let's stay with it. We might get lucky. C'mon, shark!"

"In about a minute and a half," John predicts, "Wayne's going to see a shark coming toward you, Greg." And now, at 3:42 p.m., as if on schedule, John's prediction comes true. "One's coming right toward you!" Wayne announces on the radio. "Looks like a big one, too!"

Is it the big, new shark back? Is this a different new shark? Or could it be Chex,

who we know is nearby? "I want to tag more sharks," says Greg. "But I don't want to tag Chex again. Poor Chex is a pincushion!"

Wayne is nearly out of fuel—and that means we're out of time. But what a day! We've seen at least three, and possibly as many as eight new sharks today; we've checked in via receiver buoy with Julia, and even had a sighting of Chex. It's been an immensely productive sortie for the study. Greg is happy, and our two new friends on the boat, Sebastian and Jon, are elated—as both of them tell us on our way back to shore.

Working with Ocearch in Chile, Sebastian was lucky enough to help tag and take tissue samples from fifteen sharks, mostly makos and blues. "I've only seen great white sharks on movies and videos," he says. "Seeing it live is so different. Videos take the magic out of it. Seeing it live, you feel how powerful it is, the volume of the shark."

As for Jon, he's volunteered for more than twenty-five years with NMFS's Apex Predator Program. He's caught more than 775 sharks and tagged hundreds more. "Yet I saw more white sharks today, in one day, than I did in that entire time!" he says. "I'm still wrapping my head around it."

SHARKS BY THE NUMBERS

- Estimated number of **SHARKS** (about 500 species) worldwide: **7 BILLION**

- Estimated number of **HUMANS** (just one species) worldwide: **7 BILLION**

- Number of times each year **SOMEBODY SWIMS,** surfs, or scuba dives somewhere **IN THE OCEAN:** about 15 billion

- Average number of **PEOPLE KILLED BY SHARKS** of all species yearly, worldwide: about **11**

- Number of **SHARKS** of all species **KILLED BY PEOPLE YEARLY,** worldwide: **100 MILLION**

- Number of Americans killed by **SHARK BITE** between 1984 and 1987: **4**

- Number of New Yorkers **BITTEN BY HUMANS** during same period: nearly **1,600**

- Rank of the **U.S.** in number of **GREAT WHITE SHARK ATTACKS** on people worldwide: **1**

- Rank of **SOUTH AFRICA AND AUSTRALIA** in great white attacks on people: tied for **2**

- Rank of **FLORIDA** in frequency of U.S. shark attacks: **1**

- Number of times more likely a Floridian will be killed by a **TORNADO** than a shark: **21**

- Number of times more likely you'll be killed by **LIGHTNING** than by a shark in coastal U.S.: **76**

- Number of Americans **INJURED BY TOILETS** in one year (1996): **43,000**

- Number of Americans **INJURED BY BUCKETS AND PAILS** in same period: **11,000**

- Number of Americans injured by **ROOM FRESHENERS** in same year: **2,600**

- Number of Americans injured by **SHARKS** during same time frame: **13**

- **CHANCE** of a person being **KILLED BY A SHARK: 1** in **37 MILLION**

- Chance of a person dying from the **FLU: 1** in **63**

- Number of **SHARK-DIVING BUSINESSES** operating around the world: **400**

- **AGE** to which a **GREAT WHITE SHARK** can live: at least **70**

- Number of **TEETH** a shark may produce in a lifetime: **30,000**

CHAPTER 5

FRIDAY, SEPTEMBER 26—
SUNDAY, SEPTEMBER 28

"Welcome to Guadalupe Island," says our dive master, the Mexican biologist Erick Higuera, "the best place on the planet to see great white sharks!"

That's exactly why Keith and I are here. We've flown across the country, and then braved sixteen hours of travel on ten-foot swells, to get here. Though there seem to be plenty of great whites in New England's murky green waters, it's hard to see them. (Greg tried diving in a shark cage there; he could hardly see his hand in front of his face.) But the crystal-clear waters surrounding this tiny volcanic island off Mexico, 250 miles south of San Diego, California, offer plenty of great whites and spectacular views of them.

Along with nineteen other passengers, we're on board the *Solmar V*, a 110-foot mega-yacht—just one of the boats belonging to five different companies that come here to meet the growing demand to see great whites underwater from the safety of a steel cage. We've dropped anchor a few hundred yards from the island's rocky shores. From the deck, we can see what draws the great whites: seals, sea lions, and more seals. Guadalupe is a biosphere nature reserve and sanctuary where elephant seals, Guadalupe fur seals, and California sea lions haul out and give birth to their pups.

But before we can get up close and personal with the sharks, Erick has gathered us for a safety briefing. This is not your usual scuba dive, he explains. We won't be wearing fins, tanks, or inflatable buoyancy control vests—there won't be room enough in the shark cages. There are two eight-foot-long by eight-foot-deep by five-foot-wide surface cages attached to the boat by nuts and bolts, each of which can hold four divers. In addition, there is a submersible cage, which can descend to forty feet, controlled by a crane and attached to starboard, for two passengers and one crew member.

Our portal to a sharky adventure: one of the shark cages before it's submerged.

We should be prepared for cold. The water is seventy degrees here, says Erick, which sounds warm, but water carries heat away from the body twenty-five times faster than air. So along with our masks, we'll be wearing thick neoprene wetsuits and scuba booties for warmth. Then, explains Erick, we must each don ankle weights and a harness with forty to fifty more pounds of weight around our chests. This will keep us from floating up from the bottom of the cage like weightless astronauts. Next, a crew member will attach a D ring to each diver's right shoulder, through which he'll hook the hose of a regulator, delivering our air supply. Wearing all this, we approach the cage. "Kneel, then sit, then slide forward crab-style along two metal rungs until you reach the ladder into the cage," Erick instructs us. "Twist around, face the boat, and climb down into the cage."

Sounds easy. But there are a few more things to remember:

"As you turn from left to right looking for sharks, don't turn 360 degrees," Erick tells us. Why? Because we could twist the regulator hoses up on deck, choking off our air supply. And we need to stick to our assigned corner of the cage. Weaving back and forth could tangle our air hoses like the strings of marionettes.

In front of each cage there is a wide "window" of open space, three feet long and about two feet tall, allowing photographers to fit their cameras outside the bars. "Cameras *only* outside the cage," he emphasizes. No body parts should be sticking out from the cage—for reasons we hope will be obvious soon!

And finally, "If a shark comes in the cage"—and this really got our attention— "stay away from the mouth and teeth."

"It doesn't happen often," Erick assures us. In fact, only once has a shark gotten her head in the cage here in Guadalupe, and not with this particular company. An inexpert shark wrangler lured a nine-foot great white at high speed toward the open front "window" of the cage, and the shark—rolling her eyes back into her head at the last minute, as sharks do to protect their vision—miscalculated her trajectory. She got stuck in the window opening of the cage, wedged in tight up to her dorsal fin. "Sharks don't have reverse," Erick explained, "so they thrash till the shark gets free. If it doesn't happen, we have to leave the surface cage."

"Sounds like a good idea," I whisper to Keith.

"Yeah, right after I take the picture," Keith whispers to me.

One more precaution, and that's to do with the submersible cage. Anyone can use the surface cages, but only certified scuba divers can use the submersible—not because you need your scuba skills in there, but because you might need them to get *out*. If the crane that lowers and raises the cage gets stuck, you are supposed to hook yourself up one of the emergency tanks stored there and, carrying the tank in one arm while propelling yourself with the other, swim out of the cage—past the great white sharks who have gathered around you—up to the surface to get out. "So far nothing like this has happened," Erick assures us, "but if it does, don't act like prey."

Everyone laughs. Many of us have been in hazardous situations before. In our group— seventeen men, including Keith, and four women, including me—more than a few have run with the bulls in Spain, own motorcycles, go skydiving and heliskiing, and enjoy other "extreme" sports. One guy, a locomotive engineer with a toothy moray eel tattooed on his left shoulder, has survived being run over by a train. The chance we'd encounter any of the problems Eric has outlined is remote. We

all know that what we're about to do is not dangerous—but it's certainly exciting. Diving with whites has been described as "the Mount Everest of diving thrills."

"Sharks start showing up whenever they want," Erick continues. "In five minutes, ten minutes, an hour, three hours. They're wild animals. We can't predict. Okay?" He pauses and we all nod. "Let's do it! Game on!"

Entering the cage, looking out through our dive masks, we and our diving companions see only crystalline blue. We enjoy perfect visibility for about fifty feet—but there's not much yet to see. Outside and in back of our

cage, floating in its own little cage like suet in a bird feeder, a mess of fish guts looses a bloom of blood and bits of flesh to lure the sharks. In front, we see a tuna tail on a rope, pulled enticingly through the water by the shark wrangler up top. Soon, sea creatures come to investigate: lavender fish with yellow stripes down their sides and yellow tails, called fusiliers, swim in and out of the bars; a big brown and white calico bass appears; a group of wahoo, fast-swimming relatives of mackerel, show up below. Tiny jellyfish float in and out of the cage, most of them no bigger around than coins. One stings my cheek. It doesn't hurt much. In fact, under the circumstances, it feels like a good-luck kiss from the sea itself.

Fusiliers swim inside our cage with us.

And then, everyone's attention focuses to our right. Perhaps a hundred feet away, something is happening. It seems that in an instant, the ocean itself gathers into the shape of a shark. The water has been made flesh and is swimming toward us. We can see from the claspers that this is a male.

I remember reading in the classic book *Great White Shark* the author and artist Richard Ellis's account of his experience in a shark cage while diving off Dangerous Reef in South Australia in 1985: He had waited three days until finally a great white showed up to eat the chunks of horsemeat the crew offered. The wait was worth it. The shark was both "sexy and frightening," Ellis wrote. On that dive, they were also using blood to lure the sharks. "We were drenched, bathed, showered, shampooed, awash, adrift in blood," wrote Ellis, "and still the shark swam slowly, implacably, around us." His lasting impression of that dive: "If there is one thing that is burned into your mind," he wrote, "it is the image of white teeth in a gaping mouth large enough to swallow a child."

But our shark's mouth is not gaping. Rather, he seems to be smiling. He is about ten feet long. His skin is blindingly bright: gleaming silver and cream, like a knight in white satin. He seems to move through the water effortlessly, a combination of controlled power and balletic grace. I have never seen anyone so elegant.

Closer he comes, to investigate the tuna. Now he is so close that we can see the dark dots on his snout, like freckles. These are the ampullae of Lorenzini, with which he can sense the electrical current of our beating hearts. We see his dark, ancient eye turn in its socket as he looks at the bait. But he does not lunge for it. He seems a perfect gentleman. Perhaps the shark has already eaten; perhaps he is just curious about us, as we are about him. He is not scary at all.

The great white disappears behind the boat. The largest predatory fish on earth—one who has been feared and hated for centuries—has just passed within yards of my frail human body. What do I feel? Though my heart was pounding when I descended into the cage, now, in the presence of the shark, I feel no fear. No—held in the embrace of the blue, clear sea, mesmerized by the shark's fluid beauty, I experience only an overwhelming sense of tranquility.

I am still playing the scene back in my mind when the neoprene-gloved hand of one of my fellow divers touches my left shoulder. I turn and look right, then left, then below: the shark is back again. Or is it another shark? This time he passes beneath our cage and doesn't look at us. But we get another view of the animal; now I notice what I didn't see before: something at the base of the dark dorsal fin. This shark has been tagged!

Twice more we see this distinctive shark swoop by our cage. Too soon, we hear the knock on the cage door that signals our hour below is over. It's time to return to the deck to give four other divers a chance in our cage. We can't wait to get back in again!

"My teeth were chattering, I was so excited!"

"I looked, and all of a sudden there was a shark!"

"Well, *I* couldn't see *anything*," one diver pretends to complain, "because the shark kept getting in my way!"

All of us divers are talking at once, comparing our observations. But the most exciting news comes from José Quintanilla, a master's student at Cicese University in Ensenada, Mexico. He's on board with an important mission: as part of a study like Greg's, he is identifying the sharks and marking on a check sheet the time they were seen and what they were doing. He knows the name of the tagged shark Keith and I just saw: it was Jacques—named after the inventor of the Aqua-Lung, Jacques Cousteau.

With a member of the *Solmar V* diving staff, Keith and Sy descend in the submersible cage for a deeper view.

The sharks come almost close enough for us to touch them.

Scientists at the nonprofit Marine Conservation Science Institute have been studying the great whites off Guadalupe since 2000. They have cataloged more than 150 individuals since launching the photo ID study in 2002. The sharks have names such as Lucy (whose tail is tattered and whose top fin is smashed and twisted), Snow White, Nosie, Bite Face, Belt Strap (with a scar right about where a belt would be, if he were wearing trousers), and Cream Puff (a male, who would surely be embarrassed if he knew his name). Photographs of each shark from the left and the right side have been gathered into a sort of shark yearbook, like the one Greg will be creating. There's a copy on board our boat so that we can help identify them, and so that biologists can keep track of who's who, who's where, and who's where when—crucial information for monitoring the status of the great white population here.

As it turned out, we would get to see Jacques again that first day, at 11:10, 11:20—and we think we saw him at 11:40. In the larger, deeper submersible cage, at 11:30, Barry, a dentist, and Rob, the locomotive engineer, spotted and photographed a shark they believed to be Captain Hook, named for a distinctive white "hook" over the left eye that makes him look like he's wearing a monocle.

Also on our first day, Roddy, a former real estate developer from Texas, photographed what Jose thinks may be a new female, a fourteen-footer with a distinctive check mark on the left side of her tail. Those who donate photos of new animals get to name the shark they've found. If this female turns out to be new, Roddy wants to name her Brooklyn after his niece. If the shark Rob and Barry saw is not Captain Hook but someone new, Rob wants to name him Nitro.

Every evening, the visitors who photographed and filmed the sharks go over their images with José, trying to identify each shark. "See, it's a male, the claspers here," José says to Rob and Barry. " . . . I will look for this triangle here," he says, pointing to the shape of a white patch near the gills of the shark Rob thinks might be Captain Hook. "It's like a puzzle piece."

Slowly, and with the help of visitors like us, researchers are putting together the puzzle. Our group logged thirty shark sightings on our second day, but all those sightings were of only four individual sharks. We recognized Jacques from the tag on his dorsal. We met Mike at 7:20 a.m. He came within two feet of us, circled, dived deep, then soared up and took the bait, lunging out of the water. Mau, who is about seven feet long, came at 10:35, 11:17, 11:30, and 12:40. His dorsal fin is cut off at the top. And Micks, with a distinctive W-shaped scar on the left side of his tail, showed up at 2:00 p.m.

In our three days of diving, we would log more than seventy sightings and see seven individual sharks in all, including the large female Roddy photographed (José tells us he will check with other biologists to make sure she is new).

Though some people have voiced worries that commercial cage diving could be "training" sharks to associate humans with food,

This shark seems curious about us.

shark scientists, including Greg, feel this fear is unfounded—as long as divers don't physically hand the food to the sharks. In fact, instead of the people altering the sharks' behavior, what happens on cage dives like ours is that the sharks change the people who meet them—sometimes profoundly.

Everyone on the trip seemed to agree with the sentiment voiced by twenty-four-year-old McKenna, who came on the trip with her dad. On earlier dives in different places, she told me, they'd seen "little nurse sharks—but it was nothing like *this!*" McKenna thought she'd be nervous in the water with the great

white sharks. "But it was the opposite," she said. "It was calming. And humbling.

"Having seen them," she continued, "my yearning to protect them has definitely grown. Now I would absolutely love to do something for great white conservation. I'd love to see them thriving."

THE ATLANTIC WHITE SHARK CONSERVANCY AND THE GILLS CLUB

Forty-one-year-old Cynthia Wigrin proclaims she loves "everything in nature . . . from whales to chipmunks." But, she admits, she has a favorite, as you might guess when she sweeps her long dark hair aside and reveals the tattoo on her left shoulder: "I live for the sharks for sure!"

Though she'd earned a degree in wildlife management, Cynthia ended up working for an online trading company. Then, on a vacation in South Africa, she and her husband, Ben, met great white sharks up close—and her life changed forever.

She had met wild sharks before. Certified as a diver six years earlier, she had swum with other species of sharks on dives in Nicaragua and Mexico; she had snorkeled with humpback whales in the Dominican Republic. But great whites, she knew, would be different.

From the safety of a cage, she watched the great whites come so close, they looked her in the eye. "I don't know what it was about this species. It was very clear it was aware of our presence and checking things out. I was right up close to them. There was no sense of fear, just elation. I felt like a little kid at Christmas. It felt magical."

Inspired to learn more, Cynthia discovered Ocearch's work with Greg on great whites, right

in her home state of Massachusetts. She decided to call Greg up on a July day in 2012. They talked for an hour and a half. She was amazed when she found out that while the state of Massachusetts pays Greg's salary, all the rest of his expenses for the great white study—boat, fuel, equipment, spotter plane—must be funded by donations and grants. "What can I do to help you?" she asked Greg.

"Start a nonprofit," he said, joking.

Instantly, she began working on doing just that.

She quit the job she'd had for thirteen years. She moved to the Cape. She filed the paperwork for her new organization, the Atlantic White Shark Conservancy, that October. The new nonprofit was operating by December 2012. Holding events, selling shark-themed merchandise, and organizing a website, in its first year, the Conservancy managed to contribute a major portion of the money Greg needed. The following year, it raised all the funds for Greg's study for the year.

Cynthia didn't stop at fundraising. She wanted to inspire others to care as much about

conserving white sharks as she does. "At every event we held," she explained, "a little girl"—a different one each time—"would come up to me and tell me how much she loved sharks. It was incredibly impressive to me." But she discovered a lot of the girls she met didn't have anyone else they knew who shared their interest; they were told "only boys like sharks."

Cynthia knew that's not true: "While working with Ocearch, I met a scientist who was pregnant—doing ultrasounds on pregnant sharks! I thought, I'd love to connect girls with what they could potentially do with sharks." She resolved to create a newsletter and an online discussion forum for girls who love sharks. Her seven-year-old nephew came up with the name: Gills Club.

By fall 2013 they had a logo and twelve scientists

who had agreed to participate. Now the Atlantic White Shark Conservancy emails the Gills Club newsletter to three hundred girls aged fourteen and under and more than six hundred others who are older. Their Facebook page has a thousand members. More than forty women shark biologists participate. "Our reach is across the U.S. to Australia, South Africa, and Canada," Cynthia says proudly.

Soon the newsletter was followed by monthly meetings in Massachusetts and Florida. Girls as young as five attend the gatherings, which offer talks, slide shows, films, and sometimes a chance to interact with small, live sharks who make special trips in aquaria for the occasion. "It's so exciting to the little girls involved. There's nothing like hands-on experience," Cynthia says.

"A handful of people can have a big impact," she's found. For instance, one sixteen-year-old from Cape Cod ran a stand-up paddleboard event in the town of Orleans as a fundraiser for Greg's work. She raised enough for two shark tags. "Here's a high school student who got involved on her own and made a difference—and now she's a mentor to the other girls in Gills Club.

"I've always been someone who thinks anything is possible," says Cynthia. "I've completely shifted my work. Doing this is really important. I feel really inspired by the people around me—the people volunteering a ton of their time—and on top of that, I get to be out here on the water with sharks! I'm flying high."

CHAPTER 6
TUESDAY, JANUARY 6

Fast forward: It's January. Chatham is quiet. Gone are the beach towels, the scent of sunblock, the swimmers and tourists—and so are the sharks.

But whether Greg is at home with his wife, Kimberly, and kids Wilson, seven, and Eve, four, or in his office in New Bedford seventy miles west of Chatham, the great whites are seldom far from his thoughts. There's still much work to do on his study. "Winter is a critical time to analyze all the data," Greg says. And analyzing the data is, in its own way, just as exciting as being out on the water.

Though it's still very early in the study—too soon to draw firm conclusions—the findings so far suggest intriguing possibilities, important new insights, and perhaps some downright startling revelations.

In all, from June 23 to October 28, the team logged 221 shark sightings. Of course that doesn't mean they saw 221 sharks—because, as we experienced on our August shark sortie, until you review the GoPro videos, you often can't tell if you're spotting a new shark or the same shark over and over again. As it turned out, on that day our team recorded six different individuals, including Chex—five males and—the last, big shark—one female.

By now, four months after our last trip together, Greg and the team have had time to review the whole summer's worth of videos. To everyone's astonishment, they counted sixty-eight different individual white sharks! "I was surprised by the number," Greg says. "If you'd asked me how many I thought were

Greg pulls up the data on Chex's movements.

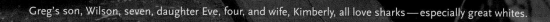
Greg's son, Wilson, seven, daughter Eve, four, and wife, Kimberly, all love sharks — especially great whites.

Because a great white shark's teeth rise forward in replicating rows, at any one time a shark may have 300 teeth in its mouth. A great white may use up to 300,000 teeth in its long lifetime.

out there, I probably would have guessed a couple of dozen." And of course, the team knows that is only a tiny percentage of the total shark population swimming in the waters off the Cape.

And this has important implications for answering one of the main questions of the study: Just how many white sharks are actually out there?

Greg has a plan to find out. "The next step," Greg says, "is to determine what proportion of the shark population we sampled." He'll need several more seasons of data. Generally, he explains, in studies like these, scientists estimate the size of a population based on the assumption that they will see and identify only three to five percent of the animals who actually live there. "If that's the case with us," he says, "then the actual number of white sharks out there could have been over a thousand."

A thousand great white sharks could be sharing the ocean with Cape beach-goers and fishermen—and, so far, rather peacefully! Who would have ever suspected?

Neither would anyone have guessed what some of the tagged sharks have revealed about their travels. At his computer, Greg pulls up the data that Lydia, one of the sharks tagged with Ocearch, has been "pinging in" this year each time she surfaces. Lydia has traveled farther north and

east than any other known great white shark ever—and turned previous ideas about white shark migration upside down. "A few years ago, everyone thought Atlantic white sharks went north in the summer and south in the winter," Greg says. And in fact, most do. Katherine, for instance, left the Cape in the fall and followed the coastline south, diving between the surface and the bottom, less than six hundred feet below.

But not all sharks conform to this pattern. Over the past month, Lydia has traveled from the shores of North Carolina all the way north to the chilly waters of Newfoundland, Canada. She is the only white shark ever documented to cross over the Mid-Atlantic Ridge, which is like an underwater mountain range separating the western from the eastern North Atlantic. At times, Lydia was closer to Greenland, Ireland, and western Africa than she was to the United States.

Mary Lee, too, has defied conventional wisdom, as her map shows. She has rocketed up and down the East Coast several times since her capture, traveling from North Carolina to New England to Bermuda to the Sargasso Sea and then back to New England, all between January and June.

The fact that both these females are very large suggests a tantalizing possibility: perhaps some of their wanderings could shed light on the mystery of great white reproduc-

tion. Great whites are long-lived and slow to mature. Females aren't thought to be old enough to mate until their mid- to late twenties (the males mature in their early twenties). Pregnancy lasts longer than a year. Unlike most fish and some sharks, who lay eggs, great white sharks give live birth, usually to between two and fourteen pups. But nobody has ever seen white sharks mate. Nobody knows where males and females hook up. Nobody knows where the females give birth. "Maybe we're finally going to get some answers," hopes Greg.

While the sharks are in these remote offshore waters, the pop-up satellite tags attached to their dorsal fins also record Lydia's and Mary Lee's diving depths. They reveal that these big females have plunged to depths of half a mile—areas thought to be perpetually dark and devoid of ocean life. The sharks sometimes do this several times a day.

"These movements were the most surprising," says Greg. "Why go so far and dive so deep?"

These are just two of the mysteries nobody even knew to wonder about before Greg's shark studies came up with these unexpected data.

Each summer's work refines the emerging picture of the life of the great white sharks of the North Atlantic. For instance: usually

Winter is the time to tabulate and analyze the data collected over the summer.

Greg breaks down the telemetry transmitters to use for another season.

the receiver buoys record the first shark of the summer—most often Julia—arriving along with the tourists: on Memorial Day weekend. But this year, though the tourists were on time, the sharks were late. Julia didn't show up off the Cape till two weeks later.

Most years, Greg explains, July is the peak month for shark detections. But this year, with 34,000 shark detections from twenty-three different tagged sharks, only ten percent of them had been recorded by the end of August. "This increased to about thirty percent by the end of September, and ninety-seven percent by the end of October," Greg says. "This means that most of our sharks were around in the early fall." Detections dropped off dramatically by mid-November, indicating that white sharks were leaving the area. The last tagged shark didn't leave till December 12.

Not only when, but where tagged sharks show up may change from year to year too. The summer's data shows that in July, most of the detections were north of Chatham Inlet, with a gradual shift to Monomoy and Shark Cove in August. This is also a departure from past years' trends. Usually most July detections are in Shark Cove. Why the change? Possibly, muses Greg, it's because after a cold winter and cold spring, water temperatures were slow to rise. "We noticed a slug of cold water in Shark Cove that persisted through July," Greg says. "This may have pushed white sharks further north into Orleans during that month, but this remains to be confirmed."

Greg's data will also eventually provide more detailed information about many individual sharks. From stills of the GoPro footage, he's developing a "shark yearbook" similar to the one scientists keep for the

SHARK MAPS

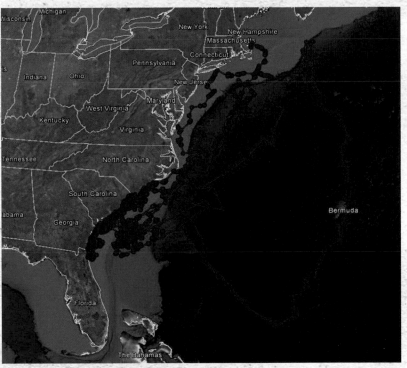

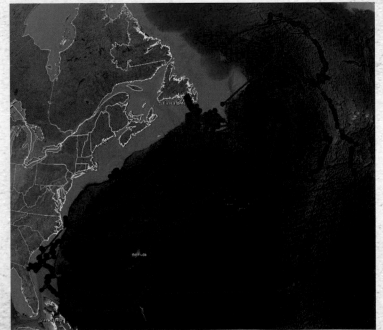

TOP LEFT: Just a little more than a year after she was tagged in August 2013 off Cape Cod, 2,300-pound Katherine had already logged 10,000 miles of travel—and much of it was through some of North America's busiest tourist waters. Katherine likes to surface, which guarantees her transmitter sends signals often.

TOP RIGHT: Mary Lee was sixteen feet long and weighed 3,456 pounds when she was tagged off Cape Cod in 2012. Her transmitter reveals she likes to hug the coast, though she has ventured as far as Bermuda.

BOTTOM LEFT: Lydia, a fourteen-footer, seems to enjoy spending time in the warm waters of the Caribbean, but then shoots north off cooler Canadian shores. She can swim hundreds of miles in one day. She's the first shark documented to make a trans-Atlantic crossing. Sometimes she doesn't ping in for weeks.

sharks off Guadalupe Island. Eventually, he'll have not only photos, but portraits of these sharks' comings and goings, with information such as whether they stick to favored "neighborhoods" or regular schedules.

We know now, for instance, that Chex has returned to the Cape year after year since he was first tagged on July 9, 2012. "Chex can be characterized as more of an Orleans shark," says Greg; Chex spent most of his summer north of Chatham Inlet, off Nauset. He did make occasional visits to Shark Cove, but didn't stay long; he stopped by between 1:30 and 5:00 a.m. on July 27, but then headed north again. He stuck around Nauset until September 20 at 10:00 a.m. The next day, he was detected more than twenty miles north, off the beaches of Truro, where he seems to have stayed until September 23 at 9:00 p.m.—after which no more detections were recorded. He must have left the area, presumably for points south. "We hope to see him next summer," Greg says.

All in all, it was an incredible field season: the team tagged eighteen sharks (including retagging Chex)—six with acoustic tags, four with pop-up satellite archival transmitting tags, and eight with both. We'll have to wait for the information from the pop-up tags; they won't detach and pop up for another year. Meanwhile, along with thousands of fans around the world, Greg continues to follow the Ocearch great whites on the Shark Tracker. And he is eager to hear from colleagues both north and south to see whether sharks with acoustic tags have "pinged in" on their receivers.

It'll be worth the wait, he's sure. "There's got to be a lot more going on than we think," Greg says. "Nothing surprises us anymore. The longer we study them, the more we learn these fish do things we could never anticipate."

Science demands patience. It may be many years before Greg can accomplish his main goal: "to tell the *real* story about sharks." That will be a tall order—and not just because there's still so much to learn. There's much to *unlearn* as well. The old, false stories, about sharks as bloodthirsty killers chomping their way through swimmers, die hard. Too many TV shows, movies, video games, and books combine a natural fascination with these large, graceful, predatory fish with fear. "Sadly, fear sells and sharks sell—combine the two and you've got something that *really* sells," Greg says.

Greg is hanging his hopes on the next generation. "Kids, including my own, are fascinated by sharks, and that in and of itself is a good starting point," he says. "Children are hungry for information. The more they know about sharks, the less they fear, the more they are fascinated, and the better our future—and that of the sharks."

BE SHARK SMART!

The country of South Africa ran a series of TV ads a few years ago to reassure people about great white sharks. One starts out showing a pleasant day at the beach. Soon the scene turns scary and finally breaks out in panic. A horrible thing has been spotted in the waves. Bathers race from the water screaming. Viewers' hearts pound as the camera pans back to the sea to reveal the source of all the terror. It's . . . a . . . toaster!

Yes, the year the ad aired, 791 South Africans were killed by malfunctioning toasters. Four were killed by sharks.

If you're not scared to enter your kitchen, you shouldn't be scared to swim at the beach. To make extra sure you're safe in the water, the U.S. National Park Service and the Towns of Cape Cod offer this advice:

- Don't swim near seals (it's illegal to harass them, and they have sharp teeth, too).

- Don't swim too far from shore (a good idea to keep from being swept out to sea).

- Don't swim or surf alone (excellent advice if you don't want to drown).

- Avoid areas where many fish are congregating and sea birds are diving (don't swim with the menu!).

- Avoid wearing shiny jewelry in the water (could look like fish scales to a shark).

- Avoid cloudy water (where a shark might mistake you for prey).

SWIMMERS AND WADERS CAUTION

DANGEROUS CURRENTS

RIP CURRENTS are strong, swift-moving channels of water rushing from the shore out to sea that can form anywhere. Look for foamy, sandy, choppy water, or water traveling seaward through an area of little wave activity. People entering shallow water can be caught in rip currents and quickly pulled out into deep water.

IF YOU ARE CAUGHT IN A RIP CURRENT:

➤ Stay calm. ➤ Swim parallel to the beach until you are out of the current, then swim toward shore with incoming waves. ➤ If you need assistance, wave your arms and yell for help.

SHARK ADVISORY

Great white sharks live in these waters.
Sharks prey on seals.
Avoid swimming near seals.

FOR YOUR SAFETY

➤ Sand collapses easily. Do not climb slopes or dig holes deeper than knee level.
➤ Be aware of changing tides and weather conditions.
➤ Watch your children at all times, and keep them within easy reach.
➤ Stay hydrated and avoid overexposure to the sun.
➤ Notify lifeguards in case of emergency.

BEACH RULES

➤ Fires require a permit.
➤ Pets must be on a leash. Pet closures may be in effect to protect shorebirds.
➤ Metal detectors are prohibited.
➤ Saltwater fishing requires a license.
➤ Camping is not permitted.
➤ Leave no trace -- carry out what you bring.

RESOURCE PROTECTION

WE SHARE THE BEACH with birds and other wildlife that depend on this undeveloped shoreline for feeding, rest, and reproduction. Watch birds from a distance and follow regulations about dogs and kites. Keep wildlife wild by not feeding, and by removing food trash that attracts predators.

Low Hazard! Medium Hazard! High Hazard!

Town of Wellfleet
Beach Warning Flags

SATURDAY JUNE 28th 5-9PM
FREE
LIVE BANDS
WELLFLEET MA

RIP CURRENTS
¡ESCÁPESE DE LA CORRIEN

WELLFLEET

SELECTED BIBLIOGRAPHY

Barbo, Theresa Mitchell. *Cape Cod Wildlife.* Charleston,
    S.C.: History Press, 2012.

Castro, Jose I. *The Sharks of North America.* New York:
    Oxford University Press, 2011.

Eilperin, Juliet. *Demon Fish: Travels Through the Hidden
    World of Sharks.* New York: Pantheon, 2011.

Ellis, Richard, and John E. McCosker. *Great White Shark.*
    Redwood City, Calif.: Stanford University Press, 1995.

Skomal, Greg. *The Shark Handbook.* Kennebunkport,
    Maine: Cider Mill Press, 2008.

WEB RESOURCES

Atlantic White Shark Conservatory: Keep up with sharky news, fundraising opportunities for Greg's work, merchandise, and the Gills Club: www.atlanticwhiteshark.org

Massachusetts Division of Fisheries: Greg contributes occasional blogs and updates on his work here: www.mass.gov/eea/agencies/dfg/dmf/programs-and-projects/shark-research.html

Ocearch: Track white sharks and others outfitted with real-time telemetry: ocearch.org

Rethink the Shark: Watch the funny (but true) TV ads created for the campaign to show what little risk great whites really pose in South Africa: www.lesleyrochat.com/conservationist/campaigner/rethink-the-shark

Stop Shark Finning: How many people are killed by sharks versus how many sharks are killed by people? Take a look at this shocking infographic. Be sure to scroll ALL the way down: www.stopsharkfinning.net/shark-attack-infographic

ACKNOWLEDGMENTS

Whether photographing the boat below from a small plane, or trying to take notes while riding tall waves, researching and photographing this book was a great adventure. For inviting us along on their exciting shark sorties, we thank our hero, Greg Skomal; our captain John King and his first mate, Pam; the Atlantic White Shark Conservancy founder and director Cynthia Wigrin and her husband, Ben; the shark biologist Jeff Kneebone; and our "eyes in the sky," the pilot Wayne Davis. For sharing their expertise and great company on our last Cape Cod foray, we also thank Jon Dodd and Sebastian Kraft.

We'll never forget our expedition to Guadalupe Island and the white sharks we met there. We'd like to thank the biologist Erick Higuera and the other fine staff of the *Solmar V*, the budding shark biologist José Quintanilla, and all our fellow divers on that fantastic trip.

We'd not be able to share the adventure with you if it weren't for still more great people helping us on land. We thank Mary Gamerman for hosting us at her beautiful home, and we thank Jody Simpson for introducing us. We thank Jan and Dave Liddell for feeding us both a great dinner and regular doses of shark news from the Cape. We are indebted to our wonderful editor, Kate O'Sullivan, for her support and advice. We're grateful to Cara Llewellen for her design expertise. And for her lovely artwork for the shark diagram, we'd like to thank Mariah Mordecai.

Finally we want to thank the great white sharks we met: off the Cape, Chex, the four other males, and big female (who are as yet unnamed—the names will be selected by benefactors sponsoring Greg's research), and off Guadalupe, Jacques, Mike, Mau, Micks, Monkey, Nitro, and Brooklyn.

A note on how this book was researched and photographed:

The stories and images in this book were gathered over hundreds of hours in the field—in the sky, on the sea, and in the water. All the events described in this book really happened, and happened just as they are described. All the photographs of wild animals were taken in a natural habitat. None were altered, manipulated, or changed.

INDEX

Page numbers in **bold** refer to photos.

SCIENTISTS IN THE FIELD
WHERE SCIENCE MEETS ADVENTURE

Check out these titles to meet more scientists who are out in the field—and contributing every day to our knowledge of the world around us:

Looking for even more adventure? Craving updates on the work of your favorite scientists, as well as in-depth video footage, audio, photography, and more? Then visit the new Scientists in the Field website!

WWW.SCIENCEMEETSADVENTURE.COM